GENERATIONAL
RANKS

BUILDING AND
TRANSFERRING
MILITARY FAMILY WEALTH

CREATE A LEGACY PLAN THAT
BUILDS GENERATIONAL WEALTH
AND FINANCIAL EDUCATION

ASK ANTWAUN

Generational Ranks

Building and Transferring Military Family Wealth

ISBN: 979-8-9936505-5-5

Published by AskAntwaun Media

All inquiries: AskAntwaun@gmail.com
Printed in the United States of America

Book Design by Williams DocuPrep
www.williamsdocuprep.com

Table of Contents

Acknowledgements

To every service member, veteran, and family who's ever wondered if financial freedom was really possible, this is for you. You've sacrificed, served, and endured. You deserve more than stability; you deserve prosperity.

To the agents, lenders, and mentors who continue to serve our military community through education and integrity, thank you. You make the difference between a buyer and a believer.

And to my family, for your patience, support, and faith during every late night, long call, and new project, you're the "why" behind every word.

Introduction

The Legacy Mission

Legacy isn't just what you leave behind. It is also what you build into the next generation while you are still here. For years, I thought wealth was a number, a certain balance in your bank account. But the longer I worked with families, especially military families, the clearer it became wealth without systems dies in one generation.

Most service members know how to fight for their country. Few are taught how to build for their family. We spend decades learning discipline, leadership, and teamwork, but when it comes to money, we often leave those same skills at the door. This book changes that.

Generational wealth isn't reserved for the rich. It is a mindset. It is structure. It is mission planning applied to money. You already know how to run a squad, manage a schedule, and execute a mission under pressure. Legacy building is no different. The only difference is the battlefield.

Every chapter in this book is a mission brief. You will learn how to set your family up like a command team, each person with clear roles, shared objectives, and a long-term strategy.

We will talk about teaching kids the value of a dollar, turning side hustles into family assets, setting up trusts to protect what you have earned, and building systems to make sure your family wealth lasts longer than you do. This is not theory; it is fieldwork.

You will see how everyday moves like buying the right home, setting up automatic savings, or naming the right trustee can stack over time into generational power. And every chapter ends with a "Family Finance Drill," a real, actionable step you can take before the next page.

Because here is the truth: If you do not teach your kids about money, the world will, and it will not be the same lesson. You have already mastered structure, strategy, and sacrifice. Now it is time to apply those same tools to your family's financial legacy. This is your next mission. And it starts here.

Chapter 1

The Family Formation Brief

In the military, every mission starts with a brief. Everyone knows the plan, the objective, and their role. That structure keeps the mission moving, even when chaos hits. But when it comes to family finances, most people operate on vibes. Money comes in. Money goes out. There's no chain of command, no mission brief, and no accountability. That stops here.

If you've ever said, "We make good money, but I don't know where it goes," this chapter is your wake-up call. We're going to treat your home like a mission because it is one. This is how you take your family from surviving to strategizing.

1. Mission Objective – Define What "Winning" Means

If you don't define success, you can't hit it. Every family's version of "winning" looks different, and that's okay. The point is to get everyone rowing in the same direction.

Start with a 10-Year Family Vision Drill:

1. Gather the family (no distractions, no TV).

2. Ask: "What does success look like for our family in 10 years?"

3. Write down what everyone says, don't correct or filter it.

4. Combine it into one statement.

Example:

"The Hill Family builds wealth through ownership, service, and discipline."

That sentence becomes your mission statement. Put it somewhere visible, on the fridge, in your office, or as your phone wallpaper.

From now on, every decision, whether spending, saving, or investing, has to align with that mission.

2. Chain of Command – Clarity Beats Confusion

In every successful unit, roles are clear. When everyone knows their lane, things move faster and smoother. Families need that same clarity.

Here's how to build your Financial Chain of Command:

Role	Duties	Example
Commander (Strategist)	Sets goals, reviews finances monthly, and decides long-term priorities.	Usually one partner— though if you're solo, you wear this hat automatically.
XO (Operations)	Manages daily money moves— pays bills, tracks accounts, manages subscriptions.	Great fit for whoever handles details best.

Intel Officer (Research)	Finds better deals, studies investment options, and stays updated on benefits.	One person researches, everyone benefits.
Quartermaster (Supply)	Handles household logistics—shopping, maintenance, and cost control.	Even kids can help here. Give them a "budget brief."

The goal isn't titles; it's teamwork. Even if it's just you and your spouse, this chart prevents the "I thought you paid that bill" conversation.

Execution Tip: Write the names next to each role on a sticky note or whiteboard. Once it's visible, it's official.

3. The Weekly Wealth Brief – Keep Communication Tight

If your family only talks about money when something goes wrong, that's a problem. You wouldn't wait until a mission failed to debrief; you'd meet regularly to stay aligned.

Set up a Weekly Wealth Brief.

- When: Once a week, same day, same time (Sunday nights work best).
- Where: Kitchen table, living room, or even a quick call if you're deployed.
- Length: 15 minutes max.

Agenda:
1. **Last Week's Objective:** What did we try to accomplish? (Save $100, pay off a card, meal prep to save $50.)
2. **Wins:** What worked? (Celebrate progress. It keeps morale high.)
3. **Intel Update:** Any new info? (Upcoming PCS, raise, deployment pay, etc.)
4. **Resource Check:** Where are we financially right now?
5. **Next Week's Objective:** What's the next small, clear goal? No guilt. No judgment. No blame. Just forward movement.

Ask Antwaun Tip:
If your spouse isn't into money talk,
start small—five minutes, one goal.
Let results sell the process.

---

4. Battle Rhythm – Systems That Run Themselves

The strongest families don't rely on motivation, they rely on systems. You already know this from military life: systems keep things moving, even when you're exhausted.

Here's how to create your **Family Financial SOPs** (Standard Operating Procedures):

System	Your SOP
Bills	All bills auto-pay from one account on the 1st and 15th.
Savings	10 percent of all income automatically transfers to savings each payday.
Investing	$50 per month automatically goes into TSP, IRA, or brokerage account.
Allowance / Family Pay	Kids "earn" allowance for responsibilities; apply 50/30/20 split (spend/save/give).

| Meetings | Weekly Wealth Brief every Sunday at 6 p.m.—non-negotiable. |

Once written, these SOPs are law. When money becomes routine, emotions stay out of the driver's seat.

5. Family Finance Drill – Activate The Formation Plan

Before the next chapter, your mission is to get your family financially aligned.

Checklist:

1. Hold your first Family Vision Drill.

2. Write your mission statement.

3. Assign your Financial Chain of Command roles.

4. Create 3–5 SOPs that make sense for your household.

5. Schedule your first Weekly Wealth Brief.

Even if it's messy the first time, that's okay structure gets better with reps. The point is progress, not perfection.

The Bottom Line

Structure builds strength. If your family doesn't plan its mission, someone else will plan it for you.

Chapter 2

Teaching Wealth Early

Most parents say they want to give their kids a better life. But a "better life" isn't built by buying more toys or bigger vacations; it's built by teaching them how to handle money.

Financial literacy isn't just about dollars and cents; it's about values. It's discipline, patience, and understanding how to turn opportunity into ownership. The earlier your kids learn this, the stronger their foundation will be.

In the military, we don't just tell new recruits what to do; we train them to think. The same principle applies to raising financially ready kids. Don't just give them money; give them the mission.

Step 1: Give Money Purpose

Children learn best when they see results. Instead of handing out allowance without meaning, break it into categories. The classic 50/30/20 rule (Spend/Save/Give) teaches balance.

Here's a simple example:

Category	Purpose	Example
Spend 50%	Everyday choices	Snacks, games, small purchases
Save 30%	Long-term goals	Bigger items, savings account
Give 20%	Generosity	Charity, church, gifts

Start with cash when they're young, physical money makes it real. As they get older, move to debit cards with parental controls like Greenlight or FamZoo to introduce digital tracking and budgeting.

When they can see their balance move after a purchase, it teaches immediate cause and effect. Explain that every dollar has a job just like every soldier has a role. Money doesn't just sit idle; it either works for you or against you.

If your child earns $10 for chores, sit with them and talk through what each dollar will do. Ask questions like, "What's your money's mission this week?" It sounds small, but it plants the seed of intentional financial thinking, the kind that turns spenders into planners.

Step 2: Introduce the Paycheck Mindset

When they earn money whether from chores, grades, or small jobs teach them to "report for duty" with their finances. Each pay cycle (weekly, biweekly, or monthly), sit down together and walk through what came in, what went out, and what stayed.

This isn't just allowance; it's training. When they learn to track income early, they'll be more prepared for their first military paycheck or civilian job later. Show them your

LES (Leave and Earnings Statement) and break it down like a mini financial map. Explain how taxes, BAH, and TSP contributions all play a part in your overall paycheck. Then, help them apply that same logic to their own money, whether it's a small allowance or babysitting cash.

For example, if your teenager makes $200 from a part-time job, show them how to divide it into categories, track it in a simple spreadsheet, and even set savings goals. The point isn't perfection; it's awareness. You're teaching them to think like a paycheck commander, not a paycheck passenger.

Step 3: Build Credit Before They Leave the House

Credit isn't something to fear it's a tool. But without guidance, it becomes one of the easiest ways for young adults to derail their financial stability. That's why credit education should start before your child ever swipes a card.

Here's a roadmap for setting them up early:

Action	When to Start	Impact
Add them as an authorized user on your credit card	13–16 years old	Builds credit history early
Teach how credit works — utilization, on-time payments	Any age	Builds habits before responsibility
Open their first secured or student card	18+	Introduces accountability with limits

When they're ready, explain how a credit score works and why it matters. Break down terms like "utilization," "interest rates," and "payment history" using real-life examples. For instance, show them how maintaining a $50 balance on a $500 card keeps utilization at 10%, which helps credit grow faster.

For military parents, use your own VA loan or car purchase as a teaching example: "See how my credit helped us qualify for this rate? That's why we protect it like mission intel."

Step 4: Connect the Lessons to Real Life

Kids learn more from what they see than what they hear. Let them be part of the process when you budget, pay bills, or discuss investments. Even if they don't understand the numbers yet, they'll start to understand the behavior.

Explain BAH, paychecks, or PCS moves in simple terms. When you move to a new duty station, show them how housing costs change and how the family adjusts the budget. If you own property, walk them through how rent or mortgage payments work and why equity matters.

The goal isn't to make them experts; it's to make money a normal conversation. In most families, money is taboo or stressful. But in yours, it can be a regular topic of teamwork.

Every discussion builds comfort and confidence that will carry into adulthood.

Family Finance Drill

This week, host a Family Payday Briefing. Give your child (or the whole family) a mock paycheck and work together to allocate it using the 50/30/20 method. Discuss why each category matters and what goals they could work toward.

If your kids are older, have them calculate how much they'd earn from a part-time job or summer internship and how much they'd save if they followed the same system. Bonus exercise: have them create a "pay stub" that tracks deductions, savings, and spending. It's a fun and visual way to reinforce the paycheck mindset.

The Bottom Line

If you can teach your child to think like a leader with their money before they ever join the workforce, you've already broken the cycle that keeps most families stuck.

Financial readiness isn't just about earning; it's about understanding. The goal isn't to raise kids who know how to spend. It's to raise future adults who know how to build.

You're not just preparing them for their first job; you're preparing them for life. And that's a legacy that lasts longer than any paycheck.

Chapter 3

The Power of Transparency

Most families avoid talking about money because they think it causes tension. But silence is the real problem. When money becomes a secret, it creates confusion, fear, and missed opportunities. When money becomes a conversation, it creates unity, discipline, and trust.

Financial transparency isn't about revealing every dollar; it is about creating a shared understanding of how your family earns, spends, saves, and builds. It turns money from a private stress point into a public mission.

Step 1: Create a Shared Financial Picture

Every family should know the basics:

- What comes in each month.
- What goes out.
- What goals you're working toward.

You don't have to share every detail with your kids, but they should understand the "flow" of money how income supports priorities.

Role	Responsibility	Example
Parents	Command & budgeting	Track income, expenses, savings
Teens	Tactical execution	Manage part-time job or allowance budgets
Kids	Observation & habit-building	Learn through weekly "money check-ins"

Transparency creates buy-in. When everyone sees how the household works, they take more ownership in protecting and improving it.

Step 2: Normalize Money Talks

Money shouldn't only come up during emergencies or tax season. Schedule monthly financial briefings in the same way you'd hold mission updates. Keep them short, structured, and predictable.

Sample "Family Finance Brief" Agenda:

1. Review last month's spending and savings.
2. Update progress toward one major goal (debt payoff, investment, or emergency fund).
3. Identify one upcoming expense.
4. End with one action for everyone to complete before the next meeting.

These meetings aren't just about numbers. They teach accountability, communication, and teamwork the same principles that make strong military units thrive.

Step 3: Turn Transparency into Training

Once your family is comfortable with open conversations, take it a step further. Assign each family member a small "financial mission."

Member	Mission	Objective
Spouse	Track and categorize household spending	Improve savings by 5 % this month
Teen	Research one investment or business idea	Present at next meeting
Child	Track allowance using 50/30/20 rule	Practice delayed gratification

This shifts the tone from "Dad handles money" or "Mom pays the bills" to "We all protect the mission."

Step 4: Share Your Financial Story

Your children will learn more from your experiences than your advice. Talk about the mistakes you made, the loans you took, the credit cards you mishandled, or the opportunities you wish you'd taken sooner.

You're not showing weakness; you're showing wisdom. When kids understand that success comes with lessons learned, they grow up with both humility and confidence.

Family Finance Drill

Hold your first Family Finance Brief this week. Print or write down your top three household goals for the next 12 months.

At the meeting:

1. Share the current status (savings, debt, or investments).
2. Let everyone suggest one way to help reach those goals.
3. End by assigning next month's "financial mission."

You'll be surprised how quickly engagement builds when everyone feels informed.

The Bottom Line

Money talk doesn't divide families, secrecy does. Transparency builds trust, and trust builds legacy. When your family learns to speak the same financial language, you stop fighting about money and start fighting for it together.

Chapter 4

The Military Advantage

Every service member has access to one of the most powerful wealth-building toolkits in the country, but most never use it.

Why? Because no one ever explains how those benefits work *together.*

Your military career doesn't just provide income; it gives you systems, structure, and benefits designed to create stability. When used strategically, those same systems can build generational wealth.

This chapter breaks down how to leverage the military advantage from BAH to TSP and use what you've already earned to secure your family's future.

Step 1: Turn BAH Into a Wealth-Building Tool

Your Basic Allowance for Housing (BAH) isn't just "free rent." It's an investment fund disguised as a benefit. Most service members spend it and forget it. But if you redirect that same allowance into ownership, you're building equity every month instead of just covering someone else's mortgage.

Situation	Typical Approach	Wealth-Building Approach
PCS move	Rent near base	Buy near base using BAH to cover mortgage
Deployment	Keep renting	Rent out your home for cash flow
Separation	Start fresh	Keep the property as a long-term investment

Even a modest home, purchased and held over multiple duty stations, can become the foundation of your family portfolio. Think of BAH as seed money your job is to plant it wisely.

Step 2: Maximize Your TSP — The Built-In

Investment Plan

The Thrift Savings Plan (TSP) is your military 401(k). It's simple, powerful, and often underused.

Here's how to think about it like an investor, not an employee.

Action	Why It Matters	Real-World Example
Contribute at least 5%	Gets you full government match	You're leaving free money if you don't
Choose Roth for long-term tax freedom	Pay taxes now, grow tax-free later	Ideal if you expect higher income post-service
Review allocation yearly	Aligns with risk and goals	Younger = more stocks; nearing retirement = more bonds

If you start early, even small contributions compound massively over time. A service member investing $300/month for 20 years at 8% return builds roughly $165,000 that's before matching and raises.

Your TSP is the silent wealth builder in your ranks.

Step 3: Use Your VA Loan Strategically

Your VA Home Loan isn't just for buying your "forever home." It's a lifetime benefit designed to help you build equity and stability at each duty station.

Opportunity	Strategy	Outcome
PCS orders	Buy instead of rent	Build equity during your tour
Outgrowing a home	Rent it out, use entitlement on next property	Grow portfolio without selling
Rates drop	Refinance with IRRRL	Lower payments or shorten loan term

Every PCS can become a stepping-stone if you plan it right. Buy with a long-term mindset something rentable, in demand, and manageable from a distance.

You can turn a 20-year career into a 4-home portfolio without ever needing a conventional mortgage.

Step 4: Leverage COLA, BAS, and Bonuses Intentionally

It's easy to treat COLA (Cost of Living Allowance), BAS (Basic Allowance for Subsistence), or bonuses like extra cash but those are wealth accelerators if you redirect them with purpose.

Allowance	Common Mistake	Smart Play
COLA	Lifestyle inflation	Save or invest half each pay period
BAS	Treated as grocery money	Automate part into savings
Bonus pay	Spent immediately	Split 50/30/20 – debt, savings, investment

The mindset shift: treat every extra allowance as temporary income, permanent opportunity.

Step 5: Build a Benefits Battle Plan

Once you understand the tools, you need a system to coordinate them just like mission planning. Here's a sample *Military Family Wealth Strategy Checklist* to use annually:

Category	Action
BAH	Owning or investing at each PCS
TSP	Contribute 5–15% with Roth allocation
VA Loan	Reuse entitlement or assume opportunities
COLA/BAS	Automate 20–50% to investments
Insurance	Review SGLI, disability, and family coverage
Retirement	Calculate projected pension + investments

This quick review each year keeps you mission-ready for every financial move.

Family Finance Drill

This week, sit down with your spouse or family and map your current military benefits on paper. List each one—BAH, BAS, COLA,

TSP, and VA Loan—and note how you're currently using it. Then identify one area where you're leaving money on the table.

Commit to improving just that one benefit over the next 30 days. Maybe it's increasing TSP by 2%, researching your VA loan options, or automating part of your COLA into savings. Small moves compound into large gains the same way small missions win big wars.

The Bottom Line

The military already gave you structure, leadership, and benefits most civilians would envy. The difference between the service member who retires comfortable and the one who retires wealthy isn't rank; it's strategy.

You've earned the advantage. Now it's time to use it.

Chapter 5

The Family Business Blueprint

Every military family already runs like a small business. There's structure, hierarchy, logistics, and a mission. The only thing missing is the *paperwork.*

Building a family business isn't about chasing entrepreneurship for the sake of it; it's about creating a legal and financial framework that allows your effort, income, and discipline to multiply.

Whether you own a rental property, sell products online, or run a side hustle, the goal is to create something that lives *beyond your paycheck.*

Step 1: Shift from Income to Infrastructure

Most people think owning a business means you need a storefront, a brand, or a massive audience. Not true. The foundation of any business is structure, not scale.

What Most Families Do	What Wealth-Building Families Do
Operate side hustles informally	Register LLCs to separate liability and taxes
Use personal accounts	Open business checking and savings
Spend profits casually	Reinvest into systems and equipment

That structure doesn't just make you look professional it protects your assets and unlocks new advantages like business credit and tax deductions.

Think of it like chain of command: your family is the command team, the LLC is your unit, and each income stream is a mission.

Step 2: Identify Your Family's Core Competencies

In the military, every mission starts with strengths assessment. Your family business should too.

Ask:

- What are we good at as a team?
- What problems can we solve?
- What experience or access do we already have?

Examples:

- A dual-military couple could manage short-term rentals near base using their PCS experience to help others.
- A spouse with organizational skills could run a virtual admin or travel-planning business.
- A retired NCO could mentor, consult, or train younger service members using their real-world expertise.

The key isn't creating something new. It's

repackaging what you already do with discipline and monetizing it.

Step 3: Turn It Into a Family Operation

Your business isn't just an income stream; it's training ground for your kids and legacy for your family.

Role	Family Member	Example Responsibility
Commander	Parent(s)	Vision, finances, operations
XO (Executive Officer)	Spouse	Administration, scheduling, client contact
Junior Officers	Kids/Teens	Marketing, social media, bookkeeping help

This doesn't just build teamwork, it gives your kids hands-on financial literacy and the opportunity to contribute meaningfully.

Give them real responsibilities. Let them help file taxes, update the website, or record payments. Every task teaches them owner-ship.

Step 4: Build the Legal and Financial Framework

Here's what every military family business should have, even at the smallest level:

Category	Tool or Action	Why It Matters
Legal	Register LLC or S Corp	Liability protection + professionalism
Financial	Open business bank account	Keeps funds separate for taxes
Operations	Accounting software (e.g., QuickBooks, Wave)	Tracks expenses, simplifies filings
Branding	Domain + logo	Builds credibility, even for side hustles
Tax Planning	CPA familiar with military deductions	Maximizes write-offs and compliance

Bonus Tip: Start tracking mileage, home office use, and any expenses tied to the business. These small deductions can offset thousands in taxes annually.

Step 5: Establish the "Family Brand"

Your family name carries weight. Building a family brand isn't about social media fame, it's about reputation, consistency, and long-term recognition.

Consider what your family stands for.

- Do you solve housing problems for military families?
- Do you educate others on benefits?
- Do you build community through service?

Your "brand" is simply how your mission shows up in the world. Name your company accordingly, something that represents your values and story.

Example:

The Hill Family Holdings

Vision: "To create housing and education opportunities for service members and their families." Every decision after that aligns with that mission and that's how legacy businesses are born.

Family Finance Drill

Hold a Family Business Briefing this week.

1. List your family's current skills, hobbies, and interests.

2. Brainstorm how each could generate income or long-term value.

3. Assign one person to research how to register an LLC in your state.

4. Set a 30-day deadline to name your family business and open its first account.

Even if it starts small, with a single digital product or a $500 side hustle, you've now created a structure that can grow, employ, and teach your future generations.

The Bottom Line

Your family business isn't just about money, it's about control. When you own the structure that pays you, you're no longer limited by rank or salary. In the military, you serve the mission. In business, you create it. Your goal isn't to get rich quick, it's to build systems that keep paying your family long after the orders stop coming.

Chapter 6

The Trust Factor

Most families don't like talking about death especially military families. We're trained to push through, stay strong, and focus on the mission. But if you've ever seen the chaos that follows when someone passes without a plan, you know this truth:

If you don't plan your legacy, someone else will. Estate planning isn't just for the wealthy. It's for anyone who wants control over how their family is protected, their assets are distributed, and their legacy continues.

This chapter breaks down wills, trusts, and legacy planning in plain language so you can make smart moves now, not leave confusion later.

Step 1: Understand the Mission — Protection, Not Paperwork

Estate planning isn't about being morbid; it's about being mission-ready. You wouldn't deploy without orders, a chain of command, and an operations plan your family's financial legacy deserves the same structure.

Tool	Purpose	Analogy
Will	Directs who gets what after you pass	Your "operations order"
Living Trust	Holds and transfers assets without court delays	Your "mission continuity plan"
Power of Attorney	Authorizes someone to act on your behalf	Your "executive officer"
Healthcare Directive	Lists your medical wishes	Your "field manual" for care decisions

These documents don't just distribute assets; they reduce stress, protect your family, and prevent outside interference.

Step 2: Wills vs. Trusts — Know the Difference

Most people stop at writing a will, thinking they're covered. But wills go through probate, a public court process that can take months (or years) and cost thousands in legal fees. A living trust avoids all that. It privately transfers assets directly to your chosen beneficiaries.

Here's the side-by-side breakdown:

Feature	Will	Living Trust
Requires probate	✅ Yes	✖ No
Becomes public record	✅ Yes	✖ No
Protects while alive	✖ No	✅ Yes
Covers out-of-state property	✖ No	✅ Yes
Cost upfront	Low	Moderate
Cost long-term	Higher	Lower

If you own a home, rental property, or business you likely need a trust, not just a will.

Step 3: Create Your Legacy Binder

Once your plan is in place, organize everything into one easy-access system. Call it your Legacy Binder, a single place your spouse, children, or executor can find *everything they need.*

Here's what to include:

Section	Contents
Identification	Birth certificates, marriage license, DD-214
Property	Home deeds, car titles, rental documents
Financial	Bank accounts, investments, insurance, debts
Legal	Will, trust documents, power of attorney
Contacts	Attorney, executor, financial advisor, CPA
Instructions	Personal letters, passwords, funeral preferences

Make two copies: one physical (locked safely) and one digital (password protected). Update it every time something major changes: PCS, new property, new child, or new account.

Step 4: Secure the Chain of Command

The biggest failure in most family estate plans? No one knows who's in charge.

Appoint clear roles now:

- **Executor:** Executes your will or trust after you pass.
- **Power of Attorney:** Handles finances if you can't.
- **Healthcare Proxy:** Makes medical decisions if you're incapacitated.
- **Guardian:** Takes care of minors.

Don't assume your family will "figure it out." Write it down. Assign it. Review it yearly, especially after major life events or relocations.

Step 5: Protect the Next Ranks

Your goal isn't just to leave money, it's to leave *structure*. Teach your kids and heirs what's coming, why it matters, and how to manage it responsibly. You don't need to share exact numbers, but they should understand:

- The existence of a plan.
- Who they'll contact if something happens.
- What your values are behind the wealth.

Wealth without understanding becomes chaos. But when your family understands the "why" behind the plan, they'll honor it not fight over it.

Family Finance Drill

This week, schedule your first Legacy Briefing.

- List your current assets, debts, and accounts.

- Decide whether you have a will, a trust, or need both.
- Identify your executor and power of attorney.
- Start your Legacy Binder even if it's just a folder for now.

Set a goal: within 30 days, have at least your will and POA complete. That's mission readiness, not fear, but preparation.

The Bottom Line

Planning for the end isn't about death. It's about life, the life your family gets to live *because* you planned ahead. You spent years protecting your country. Now protect your legacy.

Your service taught you structure, leadership, and accountability. Estate planning is just applying those same principles to your family's future.

Chapter 7

Passing the Torch

At some point, every leader has to hand over command. In the military, we call this a change of command ceremony — an orderly, structured, and meaningful transition.

In family life, though, most people skip it entirely. They build wealth, collect assets, and make big sacrifices but never actually prepare the next generation to take over. Then, when the time comes, confusion takes the place of clarity.

If you want your legacy to last, you can't just build it you have to transfer it. That's what "passing the torch" really means.

Step 1: Prepare Your Successors Before They're Needed

You wouldn't give someone command of a unit without training them first. The same principle applies to wealth. You can't expect your kids or heirs to handle assets they've never been taught to manage.

Start early:

- Let them see your budget.
- Explain your investment choices.
- Walk them through your will or trust at a high level.

Don't make it awkward; make it standard. Say, "This is part of our family mission planning." When the time comes, they won't just inherit assets; they'll inherit understanding.

Step 2: Write Your Family SOP (Standard Operating Procedures)

Every good operation has a playbook. Your family should too. Document how things work:

- Where the accounts are held.

- Who manages each responsibility.
- What the monthly bills and investments look like.
- • What the guiding principles are for decision-making

This doesn't need to be fancy. A shared spreadsheet or binder labeled "Family SOP" is enough.

Here's an example structure:

Category	Details	Notes
Banking	Primary bank, account numbers, logins	Include bill auto pays
Investments	Broker, accounts, current holdings	Review annually
Real Estate	Properties, mortgages, renters	Include insurance info
Insurance	Policies, beneficiaries, renewal dates	Verify annually
Business	LLC details, tax filings, accountant contact	Assign backup executor

This ensures that if something happens to you, the next person can step in seamlessly not scramble through paperwork.

Step 3: Transfer Responsibility, Not Just Assets

Passing the torch isn't just about naming heirs. It's about gradually giving them responsibility. You can do this in phases:

1. **Observation:** Let them sit in on financial discussions or meetings with your CPA or realtor.

2. **Participation:** Have them take ownership of one area like paying property taxes or managing one rental.

3. **Leadership:** Step back and let them make small decisions with real impact, while you're still there to guide them.

This way, by the time they inherit, they're not starting from zero they've already been leading.

Step 4: Balance Fairness and Wisdom

One of the hardest parts of legacy is deciding how to divide what you've built. Here's the truth: equal doesn't always mean fair.

If one child has been heavily involved in the family business or properties, it may make sense for them to receive a different share or role than a sibling who hasn't. That's not favoritism; that's strategic continuity.

The best way to handle it? Transparency. Have the conversation early. Explain your reasoning. Give everyone time to process, ask questions, and understand your intent. Silence breeds confusion. Clarity creates peace.

Step 5: Institutionalize the Legacy

Wealth that survives generations has one thing in common: systems. Every successful family, military, business, or otherwise eventually creates structure that keeps the mission alive beyond individuals.

Here are a few ways to formalize your family legacy:

- **Family LLC or Trust:** Keeps assets under one umbrella with shared management.

- **Family Meetings:** Quarterly or annual "Legacy Summits" to review progress.

- **Education Fund:** Allocate a portion of income or investment returns for training, courses, or college.

- **Philanthropy or Foundation:** Channel giving into a formal family project that reinforces your values.

When you turn legacy into a system, it becomes something that lasts.

Family Finance Drill

This week host a Change of Command Brief at home. Review your family's financial SOP, explain who's in charge of what, and introduce your next generation to your legacy plan.

Then, assign one responsibility, even a small one, to a family member. It could be tracking one bill, managing a savings goal, or handling a small investment account. The goal isn't perfection; it's progression.

The Bottom Line

Leadership isn't about control. It's about continuity. When you pass the torch the right way, your family doesn't lose momentum, they gain mission clarity. You've built something worth protecting. Now teach them how to protect it, too. The true test of legacy isn't what you leave *to* them. It's what you leave *in* them.

Chapter 8

Teaching the Next Ranks

Every generation either repeats lessons or builds on them. The difference lies in what the last one *taught.* You can spend decades building a solid foundation, but if you don't train the next ranks to understand, manage, and grow what you've created, the mission ends with you.

The key to real generational wealth isn't just money. It's *financial readiness across generations.*

Step 1: Teach by Exposure, Not Lecture

Kids and teens don't learn wealth from lectures; they learn by observation. If they see you budgeting, investing, and having open financial discussions, that becomes their normal.

Start small:

- Let them sit in on your "Family Finance Brief."
- Walk them through how a bill or mortgage works.
- Explain how PCS moves, housing, or BAH connect to your family's financial goals.

The goal isn't to turn them into accountants, it's to normalize financial awareness. If they see money as something to plan, not just spend, you've already won half the battle.

Step 2: Financial Milestones by Age Group

Financial readiness, just like rank progression, should happen in stages. Each phase has its own focus and training objectives.

Age Range	Focus Area	Practical Lesson

Ages 5–9	Awareness	Introduce saving jars or a digital allowance app. Explain "earn, save, give."
Ages 10–13	Responsibility	Open a youth savings account. Show them how interest works. Involve them in family purchase decisions.
Ages 14–17	Application	Add them as authorized users on a credit card. Let them track expenses and set goals.
Ages 18–22	Independence	Guide them through opening their first checking account, building credit, and budgeting their first paycheck or BAH.
Ages 23+	Ownership	Teach them about investments, taxes, and home-ownership. Help them plan long-term goals and insurance needs.

Each milestone builds discipline, not dependency. Just like in the military, you don't give rank you *earn* it through readiness.

Step 3: Connect Lessons to Real Life

The most powerful lessons happen in motion. PCS moves, deployments, and life transitions offer perfect opportunities to teach.

Examples:
- When buying a home show them how mortgage rates affect affordability.
- When moving compare housing markets and explain equity growth.
- When investing show them compound growth on paper or an app.
- When budgeting for family trips: teach the trade-off between cost and value.

Every real decision can become a teachable moment if you take the time to explain the *why.*

Step 4: Create the "Next Ranks" Program

Turn your lessons into a structured plan for your kids. Call it your Next Ranks Training Program and run it just like a real development track.

Level	Focus	Example Task
Cadet (Under 10)	Learning	Identify coins, count change, explain needs vs wants.
Apprentice (10–14)	Practicing	Manage allowance or small budget. Track one monthly goal.
Operator (15–18)	Applying	Maintain debit card, manage mini budget, earn first job income.
Leader (19–24)	Mastery	File taxes, invest first $1,000, pay bills independently.

Set small challenges, celebrate milestones, and hold "promotion ceremonies." It makes financial literacy fun, structured, and familiar just like rank advancement.

Step 5: Reinforce the Mission Through Repetition

Financial readiness isn't a one-time talk. It's a continuous conversation. Hold recurring family meetings to review progress, goals, and wins.

Keep it simple:

- **Weekly:** Allowance review and goal check-in.
- **Monthly:** Budget talk or savings challenge update.
- **Quarterly:** Family Finance Brief (review progress, investments, next steps).

As they grow older, let them lead parts of the meeting. When they start asking *you* questions, you'll know the mission is working.

Family Finance Drill

Host a Next Ranks Training Session this week. Choose one topic—budgeting, credit, saving, or investing—and create a short "lesson of the day." Keep it 15 minutes or less.

If you have teens, let them teach the next topic. It reinforces their own understanding while strengthening leadership skills. Document progress. Over time, this becomes your family's training log, proof that financial readiness is being passed down, not hoped for.

The Bottom Line

Wealth fades when it's hoarded. Legacy lasts when it's taught. The most valuable inheritance you can give your children isn't your money, it's your mindset. Because if they know how to think like builders, they'll never have to start from scratch again.

Chapter 9

The Family Wealth Council

Every successful mission has a command structure. Every strong unit has accountability. Your family's financial future deserves the same discipline.

Most households make financial decisions on the fly; whoever pays the bills decides. But wealth that lasts generations isn't built on guesswork; it's built on organization.

That's where the Family Wealth Council comes in. It is your homegrown command team for generational success.

Step 1: Establish the Council

Think of your Family Wealth Council like

your household's board of directors. It's not about ranking, it's about responsibility.

Start by defining the seats:

- **Commander (You)**: Sets the vision and ensures alignment with family goals.

- **Executive Officer (Spouse/Partner)**: Oversees daily finances and keeps accountability.

- **Operations Officer (Teen/Young Adult)**: Tracks spending or manages one small budget item.

- **Finance Officer (Optional)**: Manages spreadsheets or apps; tracks savings goals.

- **Advisors (Trusted Family/Friends)**: May include a CPA, agent, or mentor for big-picture strategy.

The structure gives everyone a defined role, not just a voice, but a function.

Step 2: Hold Regular Briefings

The difference between a good plan and a great one is consistency. Your Family Wealth Council should meet on a set schedule, not just when there's a problem.

Frequency	Purpose	Example Agenda
Monthly	Review income, expenses, savings progress	What went right / what to adjust
Quarterly	Evaluate investments, insurance, debt, and family goals	Update the mission plan
Annually	Review full net worth, retirement progress, and legacy updates	Realign the long-term strategy

Each meeting should end with action items — who does what before the next briefing. Keep it short, keep it structured, and treat it like a mission update.

Step 3: Track the Metrics That Matter

You can't improve what you don't measure.

Set up a simple Family Financial Dashboard, one place to monitor your top priorities:

Metric	Why It Matters	Goal Example
Savings Rate	Measures consistency	Save 20% of income
Debt-to-Income Ratio	Ensures stability	Keep below 30%
Investment Growth	Tracks wealth building	7%+ annual return
Net Worth	Shows long-term progress	Increase yearly
Passive Income %	Gauges freedom progress	25% by 2030

You can track this in a spreadsheet, Notion board, or even a whiteboard on your fridge. The tool doesn't matter, the *discipline* does.

Step 4: Make the Meetings About Vision, Not Just Numbers

Money talk shouldn't feel like punishment. Your council meetings are about alignment making sure every decision connects back to the family's "why."

Ask questions like:

- "What do we want our money to do for us this year?"
- "What does financial freedom look like for our family?"
- "What new opportunities can we create with what we've built?"

Encourage everyone, even kids to contribute ideas. When they feel included, they feel invested.

Step 5: Institutionalize Accountability

Military operations use after-action reviews. Your family should too. At the end of each quarter, do a simple After-Action Financial Review (AAFR):

- What worked?
- What failed?
- What's next?

Document lessons learned and update your SOP. This ensures you're not just reacting, you're evolving.

Step 6: Celebrate Wins Like Promotions

Don't make the Wealth Council all about corrections; make it about celebration. When you hit a financial milestone such as paying off debt, hitting a savings goal, or increasing net worth, recognize it. Have a family dinner, do something fun, or write it in a "Family Victory Log." Progress deserves recognition. That's how you build morale and momentum.

Family Finance Drill

Schedule your first Family Wealth Council Briefing this month. Create a shared agenda:

1. Review your financial snapshot (income, savings, debt).

2. Discuss one short-term and one long-term goal.

3. Assign one task to each member, even the kids.

Keep minutes or notes to track consistency

over time. Your family's financial stability should be run like a unit because it *is* one.

The Bottom Line

When your family runs like a team, wealth stops being random; it becomes repeatable. The Family Wealth Council isn't about control. It's about clarity, communication, and continuity. Money doesn't build legacy; structure does. Because when everyone in the family knows the mission, the mission never dies.

Chapter 10

Golden Nuggets: The Legacy Code

Every family needs a code not just values written on a wall, but principles lived every day. Your legacy code is the operating system of your household the rules that protect, grow, and multiply your wealth across generations.

You can modify it, expand it, or personalize it, but these ten golden nuggets will give your family a foundation that lasts.

1. Mission Before Money

Never chase money without purpose. Every dollar should have an assignment, a mission tied to your goals, not your impulses. Money is the soldier. You are the commander.

2. Earn with Intention, Spend with Awareness

Earning more won't fix poor discipline. You can't out-earn bad habits. Track where your money goes because what gets tracked gets respected.

3. Save First, Spend Second

Most people wait to see what's left before saving. Builders reverse that. Treat saving like a non-negotiable bill. Pay your future first.

4. Turn Income Into Ownership

BAH, COLA, tax returns, side hustles, they all flow through your hands. Don't just collect them. Convert them into assets that grow while you sleep. Every dollar you own should work harder than you do.

5. Teach While You Build

Every decision is a lesson in disguise. Let your kids see your process, the wins, and the losses. You don't need to be perfect; you need to be *transparent.* That's how you pass down wisdom, not just wealth.

6. Protect Before You Prosper

Insurance, wills, and trusts aren't paranoia they're preparation. You can't build legacy on uncertainty. Plan like you won't be here tomorrow, even if you'll be here for decades.

7. Automate What You Can't Monitor

Systems don't sleep. Set up automation for savings, bills, and investments. Remove emotion from the process and let discipline work on autopilot.

8. Celebrate Progress, Not Just Perfection

Legacy building is slow and steady. The biggest wins are often invisible at first consistency, discipline, and communication. Celebrate the steps forward. That's how you keep morale high and mission active.

9. Build Wealth Quietly, Impact Loudly

Don't chase validation. Chase velocity. Your money doesn't need to prove anything, it just needs to perform. True legacy speaks for it-self.

10. Never Stop the Mission

Legacy isn't a one-generation goal. It's a living system that outlives you. Your role is to start the mission, train the next ranks, and make sure they're ready to continue it. The day your children say, "We're ready, we've got this" that's the moment your mission is complete.

Family Finance Drill

Gather your family and write your own Legacy Code. List your top 10 principles—what you believe about money, work, giving, and growth. Print it, frame it, and hang it where you'll see it often. This becomes your family's creed. The same way units have mottos, your family will have a mission statement that guides every generation.

The Bottom Line

Money fades. Systems endure. The Legacy

Code keeps your mission alive when you're gone. Every principle here is simple but applied consistently, it becomes unbreakable. Generations change, markets change, even the world changes but discipline, clarity, and purpose never go out of style.

Chapter 11

Conclusion: Generations Don't Wait

Legacy doesn't start when you're gone. It starts the moment you decide to take responsibility for the generations coming after you.

Too many people say they want to "leave something behind" but legacy isn't about what you leave. It's about what you build *into* the people who will carry it forward.

If you've made it this far in the book, you've already separated yourself from most. You've chosen structure over guessing, education over excuses, and systems over chaos. That's the foundation of generational wealth, and it starts right where you are.

The Mindset Shift

Building wealth isn't about greed; it's about *freedom.* It's about creating options for your children that you didn't have. It's about making sure the people who depend on you never have to start from zero again.

The truth is that the military already gave you the framework for this. You understand mission planning, accountability, teamwork, and execution. This book just showed you how to apply that same structure to your family's finances.

Now you have a new mission, one that doesn't end when the deployment does.

The System You Built

Think about what you've designed through this journey:

- You've formed your **Family Command**

Team.

- You've created financial roles and routines.

- You've started teaching wealth early, passing down habits that build confidence.

- You've protected your assets with structure: trusts, insurance, and estate plans.

- You've started building not just wealth, but *leaders* who will guard it.

That's not just success. That's sustainability.

The Legacy Test

Here's a simple test to know if your system is working: If you walked away today, could your family still run the mission?

If the answer is yes, you've already achieved what most never do. If the answer is no, your mission's not over yet. Either way, the solution is the same: keep going. Legacy is never finished; it's maintained.

Your Call to Action

Generations don't wait, and neither should you. Start today:

- Update your family plan.

- Schedule your next finance briefing.

- Revisit your "Legacy Code."

- Teach your kids something new about money this week.

The Bottom Line

Legacy isn't built in a year. It's built in daily decisions. Every budget, every investment, every conversation—it all stacks. The only question is, what are you stacking toward?

You've earned your rank, your experience, and your discipline. Now, use them to earn something greater: peace, stability, and impact that lasts long after you're gone.

Generations don't wait. And now, neither do you.

Epilogue

The Quiet Reward

There's a moment that hits you when all the noise finally quiets down. It's not when the bank account grows. It's not when the property closes. It's not even when the numbers start to prove what you built.

It's when you realize your family doesn't worry the way they used to. Bills get paid on time. Savings don't feel impossible. The conversations around money start sounding different, calmer, and more confident. That's the real reward of legacy. It's not flashy. It's quiet. It's peace.

When I left the military, I thought I was done serving. But what I've learned is that service doesn't stop; it just shifts. Now, the mission is different. It's not about defending a country. It's about defending a future.

If you've made it to this page, you've already done more than most will ever attempt. You didn't just read another book; you accepted a mission. And that mission doesn't end here. This is where it begins.

So when you close this book, don't shelve it; apply it. Start the family meeting. Have the hard talk. Build the system. Set the example.

Because every system you create, every dollar you redirect, every lesson you teach—this is how the next generation wins before they even start. That's how you create legacy.

You've built the mindset. You've built the structure. Now build the future. And if you ever need help sharpening the plan, you already know what to do.

Ready to put your plan in motion? Scan the QR code below to schedule your free 1-on-1 Strategy Session, and let's map out your next mission together.

This is your legacy. This is your next chapter. And I'm honored to walk beside you in it.

— Ask Antwaun

About The Author

 Antwaun Hill is a U.S. Army veteran and Hawaii-based real estate professional who's helped countless military families turn their benefits into wealth.

After serving 13 years in the Army and another decade as a Department of Defense contractor, he discovered a truth that changed his life: "Financial freedom isn't earned through rank; it's built through strategy."

Through his brand Ask Antwaun, he's become a leading voice in VA loan education, teaching service members how to leverage BAH, entitlement, and PCS cycles to build equity, ownership, and legacy.

His "BAH Means Buy A House" movement

has inspired thousands to stop renting, start investing, and take control of their financial missions.

When he's not helping families navigate homeownership or writing his next guide, you'll find him mentoring fellow veterans, spending time with his family, and building his own legacy one property at a time.

Need real estate answers? Just Ask Antwaun.

Other books in this series